I Love Every-People

I Love Every-People

Written by Florence Parry Heide
and Roxanne Heide

Illustrated by John Sandford

CONCORDIA®

Publishing House
St. Louis

Concordia Publishing House
Copyright © 1978 Concordia Publishing House
Manufactured in the United States of America

Library of Congress Cataloging in Publication Data

Heide, Florence Parry.

    I love every-people.
    (The Concept series; 2)
    SUMMARY: A story based on the concept of
God's commandment to love one another.
    1. Love (Theology)—Juvenile literature.
(1. Love. 2. Christian life) I. Heide, Roxanne,
joint author. II. Title.
BV4639.H34   241.6 77   77-15651
ISBN 0-570-07785-0

With much love to dearest Pop

Work People

Play People

Night People

Day People

Strange People

Friend People

Stiff People

Bend People

Fat People

Bone People

Lone People

Talk People

Still People

Plain People

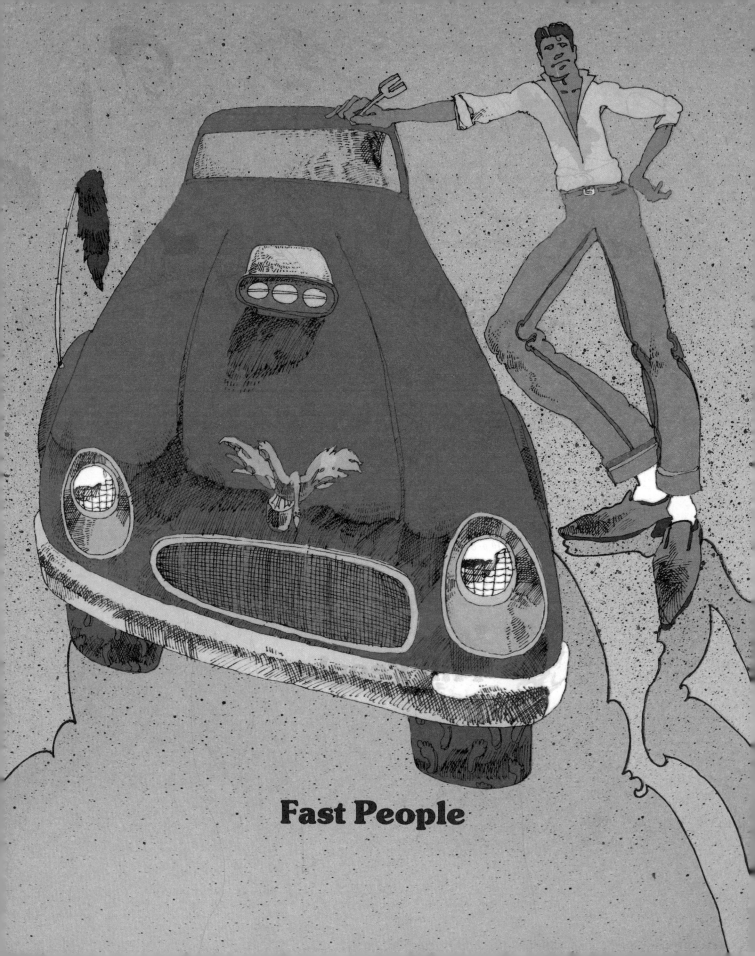

Fast People

Slow People

Stay People

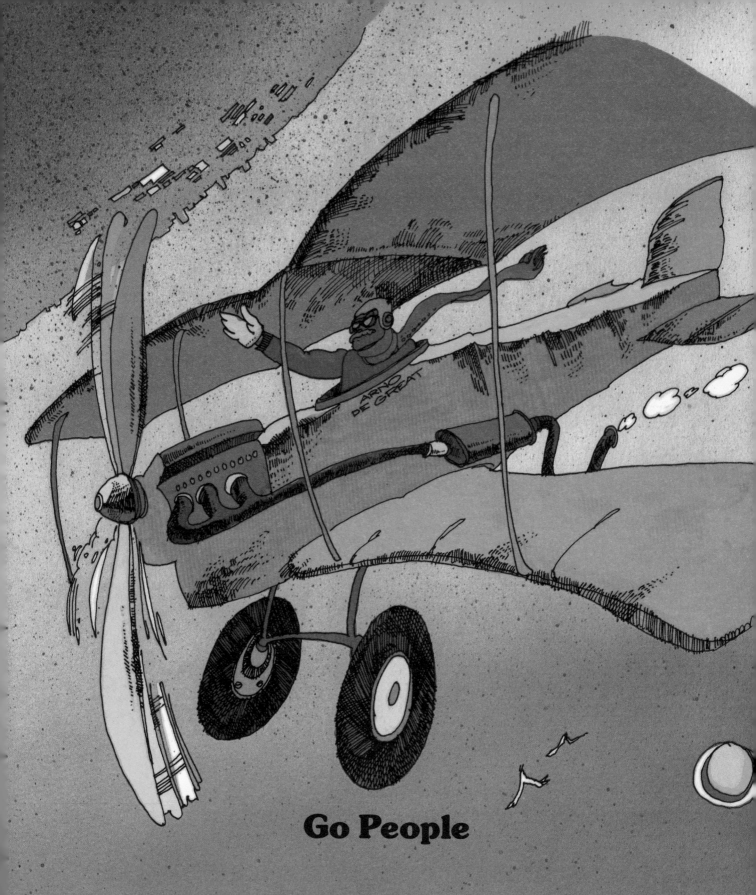

Go People

Sit People

Do People

Old People

New People

I Love Every-People

Because

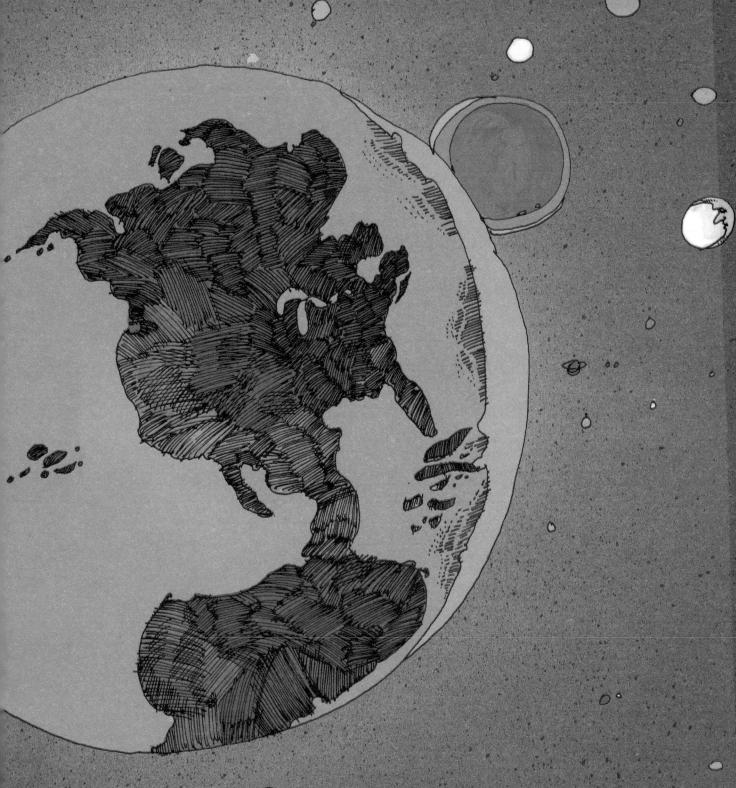

God Loves Me!